ONE HUNDRED TINY HABITS

Small Steps to Transform Your Life Every Day

The Power of Small Steps in Shaping a Fulfilling Life

Rajesh Vairapandian

INDIA • SINGAPORE • MALAYSIA

ISBN 979-8-89133-383-3

Dedicated

To

For all the silent wishes, quiet prayers, and moments of doubt.

May this book be an answer, a solace, and a guiding star.

Contents

Preface

I still remember those days when I felt adrift in the vast ocean of life, overwhelmed by the waves of challenges and doubts that threatened to pull me under. Goals seemed like distant islands, unreachable and almost mythical. It felt as if life was happening to me, rather than me being its active participant. But today, as I pen down these words, I stand testament to the power of transformation, a journey sparked and fueled by tiny habits.

Let me take you on a journey - my journey. The transformation didn't occur overnight. Nor was it the result of a groundbreaking epiphany or a once-in-a-lifetime opportunity. It was a culmination of small, consistent habits that gradually aligned my life with my aspirations. These seemingly insignificant changes, when practiced daily, became the stepping stones leading me toward my dreams.

You might wonder, how can tiny habits wield such power. But that's the beauty of it. They are unassuming, manageable, and easy to incorporate into daily life. These habits do not ask for drastic changes; they simply request consistency. And in that consistency, they weave magic.

One of the initial habits I began with was dedicating early morning self-time. In the serenity of dawn, I would reflect, meditate, and set the tone for the day. It was a small commitment but had profound ripple effects. It gave me clarity, peace, and a reservoir of energy that I could dip into throughout the day.

Similarly, it wasn't a monumental task when I chose to nourish my subconscious. It was a nightly ritual of positive affirmations and visualizations. This seemingly simple habit reshaped my internal dialogue. No longer was I my harshest critic; I became my most fervent cheerleader, believing in the realm of possibilities.

I won't pretend the journey was devoid of challenges. There were days when negativity threatened to overshadow my spirit. But by then, the habit of shielding myself from such energy had become second nature. Through affirmations, uplifting literature, and surrounding myself with optimistic influences, I fortified my defenses.

These habits, coupled with others, became my arsenal against setbacks. They guided me when I felt lost, comforted me in moments of despair, and celebrated with me in times of joy. They became my compass, leading me towards my goals, one small step at a time.

This book is an invitation - an invitation to embark on a journey of self-discovery and transformation. As you turn these pages, you'll uncover the very habits that transformed my life, each chapter a testament to the power of consistent, tiny changes. My hope is that they resonate with you, inspire you, and become your trusted companions on your own journey of growth.

Each chapter in this book is not merely a recommendation; it's a lived experience. Every practice at the end of a chapter is a tool that has personally helped me steer my life in the desired direction. I share them with you in the hope that they serve you as profoundly as they served me.

As you embark on this journey, remember, that it's not about the enormity of the change but the consistency of the effort. In these tiny habits lies the promise of a brighter, more aligned future, waiting to be unlocked by you.

I once stood where you might be standing now, at the precipice of change. I took the leap, placing my faith in these tiny habits. And today, I can proudly say they didn't let me down. They have been my allies, and my guiding stars, leading me to achievements and personal growth I once only dreamed of.

May you find in this book not just habits, but a reflection of what's possible. May it inspire, guide, and walk beside you, as you carve out the life you've always envisioned.

Wishing you a journey filled with growth, insights, and transformative moments.

– Rajesh Vairapandian

svprajesh@gmail.com

PART 1

MINDFUL GROWTH & MENTAL HEALTH

You know, there was a time when I'd find myself constantly buried under notifications, losing hours to mindless scrolling, and feeling like I was on a relentless treadmill of life's demands. Sound familiar? It's like being in a crowded room where everyone is shouting, and you're just trying to hear your own thoughts.

One evening, after a particularly draining day, I sat by my window, gazing out. The city's hustle and bustle continued below, but I had a sudden realization: I was hardly ever 'present.' I mean, when was the last time I truly tasted my coffee without thinking of the day's to-do list or just listened to a song without multitasking?

That's when I embarked on this journey of mindful growth and mental health. And let me tell you, it's been transformative. This section isn't just about meditation or those 'feel-good' quotes. It's about small, intentional steps we can weave into our daily lives to find clarity amidst the chaos. From the simple joy of stargazing to the profound effects of self-love, these chapters are like cozy evening chats, guiding you towards a more conscious, fulfilling life. So, grab your favorite mug, get comfy, and let's dive into this journey together.

Chapter 1
Cultivate Self-compassion

I was at a coffee shop a few years back when I overheard a young woman berating herself for a minor mistake at work. Her self-talk was so harsh, it reminded me of times when I had been equally cruel to myself. We often offer warmth and understanding to friends but turn into our own worst critics during personal setbacks.

One evening, during a personal reflection, I recalled a phase of life where each minor failure left me drowning in self-doubt. But then, I came across the concept of self-compassion: treating oneself with the same care and understanding as we'd offer a dear friend. This perspective shift was transformative. Instead of being trapped in a cycle of self-criticism, I started to heal, grow, and embrace challenges with renewed vigor.

Embracing self-compassion doesn't mean neglecting personal responsibility. It means allowing oneself to be human, to err, learn, and move forward. This minor shift in mindset can be the catalyst for profound personal growth.

Practice: This week, be mindful of your inner dialogue. Every time you catch yourself being overly critical, pause and ask: "Would I talk this way to a dear friend?" Redirect the conversation with yourself in a kinder, more compassionate direction.

Chapter 2

Cultivate Patience with Self and Others

During my early years, I often found myself riddled with impatience. Whether it was waiting for a bus or trying to master a new skill, the feeling of urgency was always at the back of my mind. I felt every tick of the clock as a personal challenge. One day, while waiting for a friend who was running late, I watched an old couple leisurely stroll in the park. Their calm demeanor and gentle smiles spoke volumes. The world wasn't rushing them, so why was I letting it rush me?

It's not easy, this journey of cultivating patience, especially with oneself. But I've come to realize that life isn't a sprint; it's a marathon. Every moment is a lesson, every delay an opportunity to grow. Embracing this has not only brought tranquility to my life but also enriched my relationships.

When we give patience to others, we indirectly gift it to ourselves. Because in those moments of waiting, we learn, we adapt, and most importantly, we grow.

Practice: For the next week, whenever you feel your patience tested, take three deep breaths. Remind yourself that time is a teacher, and every moment of patience is a step toward inner peace.

Chapter 3

Enhance Observational Skills

I've always been a keen observer. But often, in the race of life, I overlooked the minor details. It took a mundane evening, watching children play in the park, to truly understand the depth of observation. The laughter, the tiny wrinkles forming around their eyes, the synchronicity of their movements – it was like watching a beautifully choreographed dance.

This newfound approach made me more aware of my surroundings. It's fascinating how the world transforms when you truly look. The patterns in the falling leaves, the rhythm of raindrops, or the silent whispers of the wind; everything becomes a melody. And it's not just nature; humans, with their myriad expressions, gestures, and emotions, become an open book.

By honing my observational skills, I was not only appreciating the world more but also understanding people and emotions at a profound level. It's like unlocking a superpower, one where you see beyond the evident, diving deep into the soul of the world.

Practice: Dedicate 10 minutes of your day to sit quietly and observe without judgment. Jot down your observations and reflect on how they made you feel.

Chapter 4

Embrace New Experiences

Growing up, I was quite the creature of habit. My days were structured, my routines set in stone. But during a solo trip to China, everything changed. I found myself lost in a small village with no knowledge of the local language. Instead of panic, I felt exhilaration. I communicated through gestures, tried local foods without knowing their names, and danced to tunes I'd never heard before.

This spontaneous adventure made me realize the beauty of new experiences. The world is a vast canvas, and sticking to one corner doesn't do it justice. By stepping out of my comfort zone, I discovered not just new cultures, foods, or music, but also facets of my own personality that were previously hidden.

Embracing the unknown became my new mantra. It not only added zest to life but also made me more adaptable and resilient. After all, life is an adventure, and every new experience is a chapter waiting to be written.

Practice: This week, step out of your routine. Try a new activity, food, or even a new route to work. Note down your feelings and reflections on this fresh experience.

Chapter 5

Embrace the Power of Presence

Life has a peculiar way of rushing by, blurring moments into a continuous, indistinguishable whirlwind. It was during a serene morning, as I sat watching the sun gently rise, that I grasped the profound beauty of being truly present in the moment.

Presence is not just about physical existence in a space; it's about immersing oneself wholly in the experience. As I began practicing this art of total immersion, the mundane transformed into the extraordinary. A simple act, like feeling the texture of a page as I turned it or tasting the intricate flavors in a sip of tea, became deeply enriching experiences.

This practice of deep presence allowed me to connect with life at a more profound and meaningful level. Interactions became richer, emotions more vibrant, and experiences more memorable. The world around me seemed to respond to my heightened awareness, revealing its treasures in unexpected places.

Practice: Dedicate a moment in your day to do something with complete attention, be it sipping a drink, reading a book, or merely breathing. Feel the world around you with a heightened sense, and savor the depth it brings to the experience.

Chapter 6

Immerse in Nature

During my teenage years, the world of concrete and screens consumed me. It wasn't until a spontaneous forest trek that I felt the genuine embrace of Mother Nature. Every rustling leaf, every chirping bird, and every glistening dewdrop became a symphony to my soul. I realized that nature wasn't just around me; it was a part of me.

Being immersed in nature, away from the constant buzz and pings of the digital world, brought clarity and tranquility. The trees stood tall, teaching resilience, the rivers flowed with purpose, and the wind whispered tales of eons past. There's a reason our ancestors worshipped nature – it's healing, teaching, and uplifting.

By making nature a regular part of my routine, I gained a broader perspective on life. The challenges seemed smaller, solutions clearer, and the soul lighter. In every ripple of water, flutter of a butterfly's wing, or rustling of leaves, there's wisdom waiting to be discovered.

Practice: Dedicate an hour this week to be with nature, devoid of any digital distractions. It could be a park, a beach, or your backyard. Absorb its essence and reflect on its lessons.

Chapter 7

Seek Inner Clarity

Amid the whirlwind of life's demands, I often felt lost, like a ship without a compass. My actions lacked direction, my thoughts cluttered. One rainy evening, seated by the window, I began to introspect. I questioned my intentions, desires, and dreams. It was the beginning of a journey toward inner clarity.

Seeking clarity isn't about having all the answers but about asking the right questions. It's about aligning actions with intentions, about understanding the 'why' behind the 'what'. The clearer my inner world became, the brighter the outer world appeared.

By investing time in understanding my desires, fears, strengths, and limitations, I not only became more decisive but also more at peace. Life became a harmonious melody rather than a cacophony of confusion.

Practice: Set aside 15 minutes daily to introspect. Ask yourself – What am I feeling? Why am I feeling this way? What can I learn from it?

Chapter 8

Delve into Sensory Meditation

I once believed that meditation was purely a mental exercise, a journey inward. But then I discovered Sensory Meditation, which rooted me in the very fabric of the present, reminding me of the richness of the world around.

Every session became an exploration, tuning into the symphony of sensations around me. The whisper of the wind, the delicate aroma of blooming flowers, or the intricate dance of light and shadow – every nuance became vivid, magnified.

This practice transformed my daily life. Mundane activities like sipping tea or walking in a park became profound experiences. Each sense became a portal to deeper awareness, pulling me out of my mind's clutter and grounding me in the beauty of the moment.

The journey of Sensory Meditation isn't just about amplifying the senses. It's about experiencing life in its fullest, untainted glory, and recognizing the extraordinary in the ordinary.

Practice: Find a calm space, close your eyes, and take a few minutes to focus on one specific sense. Dive deep into the experience, noting every nuance and detail.

Chapter 9

Focus on Single-tasking

I prided myself on being a multi-tasker. Juggling emails, calls, and tasks was my daily routine. But the reality hit when I realized that while I was doing many things, I was mastering none. I decided to shift gears and embrace the power of single-tasking.

By focusing on one task at a time, not only did my efficiency skyrocket, but the quality of my work also improved. Gone were the days of scattered attention and half-done jobs. Every project, every task became a piece of art, receiving my undivided attention and care.

The tranquility that single-tasking brought was unparalleled. It reduced stress, increased productivity, and most importantly, it brought a sense of accomplishment. Life became less about the quantity of tasks and more about the quality of experiences.

Practice: Today, list down your tasks and tackle them one by one. Observe the difference in your productivity and mental state.

Chapter 10
Daily Gratitude Reflection

In the race to achieve, I often overlooked what I had. The aspirations overshadowed the accomplishments, the wants overpowered the haves. But a simple gratitude journal changed everything. Every night, I began listing three things I was thankful for. The effect was transformative.

By focusing on gratitude, my mindset shifted from one of scarcity to abundance. The challenges remained, but they seemed more surmountable. The world seemed kinder, brighter, and more promising.

The daily reflection became a beacon of positivity. Even on the gloomiest days, I found rays of hope, moments of joy, and reasons to smile. It wasn't about ignoring the challenges but about acknowledging the blessings.

Practice: Before going to bed tonight, jot down three things you're grateful for. Make this a daily ritual and observe the shift in your mindset.

Chapter 11
Embrace Shadow Work

Engaging with the hidden corridors of my mind, I stumbled upon shadow work – a transformative process of embracing and understanding the darker, unseen aspects of oneself. These are the facets we tend to hide, dismiss, or even deny. And in accepting them, I found a deeper resonance with my true self.

Walking this path wasn't always easy. The shadows often held memories, feelings, and traits that were uncomfortable. But the liberation of acknowledging them, understanding their origins, and weaving them into the narrative of my life was unparalleled.

Embracing my shadows brought another unexpected gift - a heightened sense of empathy. When you understand your darkness, you become more tolerant of others', viewing their actions and reactions with a kinder, more compassionate lens.

The journey of shadow work is profound and deeply transformative. It brings forth a version of oneself that's authentic, unafraid, and integrated, striking a beautiful balance between light and dark.

Practice: Dedicate a quiet moment each week to introspect on an aspect of your personality you've previously shied away from. Reflect on its roots and role in your life.

Chapter 12

Embrace Meditation

In a world of chaos, I yearned for serenity. Amid the cacophonous bustle, I sought silence. Meditation, initially an experiment, quickly turned into an essential part of my daily routine. The stillness of mind it provided became my anchor, grounding me in turbulent times.

With each session, I felt a connection, not just with myself but with the universe. The worries dimmed, replaced by a clarity and calmness that words can scarcely describe. It wasn't an escape from reality but a deeper dive into it.

Meditation taught me patience, self-control, and most importantly, the value of the present moment. It became my daily dose of inner peace, a journey inward to explore the vast cosmos within.

Practice: Dedicate 10 minutes today to meditation. Start simple, focusing on your breath, and let your mind journey inward.

Chapter 13

Cultivate Active Listening

I recall moments when I'd nod along in a conversation, my mind miles away. It was only when I began to truly listen – not just hear – that I realized the power of genuine engagement.

Every conversation became an opportunity: to learn, to empathize, to understand. It wasn't just about catching words; it was about tuning into the tones, the pauses, the emotions carried in those spoken sentences. Listening shifted from being passive to a dynamic, active endeavor.

Through active listening, I formed stronger connections, better comprehended emotions, and fostered deeper relationships. The world spoke, and for the first time, I felt like I was truly part of the conversation.

Practice: In your next conversation, truly focus on the speaker. Don't formulate responses in your head; just listen. Later, reflect on the emotions and insights you gathered from simply being present in the conversation.

Chapter 14

Embrace Vulnerability

There was a time when I wore an armor, shielding my true feelings from the world. Afraid of judgment and rejection, I hid behind walls, convinced they protected me. The day I decided to embrace vulnerability was the day my life took a turn.

Allowing myself to be seen, flaws and all, was terrifying but liberating. It wasn't about showcasing weakness but acknowledging my authentic self. I discovered that in my vulnerable moments, I was the most powerful. It fostered genuine connections, birthed deeper relationships, and ignited trust.

By embracing vulnerability, I not only set my true self free but also paved the way for others to do the same. It's in our raw, unfiltered moments that we truly connect, creating bonds stronger than any facade could ever achieve.

Practice: Reflect on a recent experience where you felt vulnerable. Instead of pushing it away, embrace the emotion. Discuss it with someone you trust, and notice the depth it brings to your relationship.

Chapter 15

Recite Peaceful Affirmations

The power of words on my psyche always fascinated me. One morning, during a particularly tumultuous time, I began reciting peaceful affirmations. The impact was profound. The clouds of anxiety and doubt slowly began to dissipate, replaced by a calm assurance.

Words, I realized, have the power to heal, to comfort, and to empower. By consciously choosing my thoughts and affirmations, I started reshaping my mindset, gravitating towards positivity, calm, and resilience.

The daily recitation became my shield, protecting me from negativity, bolstering my confidence, and grounding me in peace. It wasn't magic, but it felt close.

Practice: Start your day tomorrow with a peaceful affirmation. Repeat it throughout the day, especially during challenging moments, and watch its transformative power.

Chapter 16

Dive into Mindfulness Techniques

Rushing through life, I often missed its beauty. Then, I stumbled upon mindfulness, a practice that taught me to live in the moment. Every bite of food, every gust of wind, every drop of rain became an experience to be savored.

With mindfulness, life's colors became brighter, its melodies sweeter. I began to appreciate the now, understanding the impermanence of moments and the importance of cherishing them.

Mindfulness didn't just improve my mental well-being; it enhanced every facet of life. By being present, I was more empathetic, more understanding, and undoubtedly happier. Life became a series of beautiful moments, waiting to be experienced in their entirety.

Practice: During your next meal, practice mindfulness. Savor every bite, be present in the experience, and relish the flavors, textures, and aromas.

Chapter 17

Avoid Self-deprecation

There was a time when self-deprecating jokes were my defense mechanism. I believed that by making fun of myself first, I could shield my heart from the pain of others doing the same. Over time, I realized that this seemingly harmless habit was chipping away at my self-esteem, bit by bit.

Every chuckle at my own expense was a subtle reinforcement of self-doubt. The transition from light-hearted humor to genuine self-belief wasn't easy, but it was necessary. Slowly, I began replacing negative self-talk with positive affirmations and self-compassion.

This journey was transformative. It taught me that self-respect begins within. By honoring myself, I laid the foundation for others to do the same. It became less about seeking external validation and more about inner peace and self-acceptance.

Practice: Today, whenever a self-deprecating thought arises, counter it with two positive affirmations. Embrace your worth and see the change in your perspective.

Chapter 18

Engage in Mindful Listening

There's a difference between hearing and listening. I found serenity not just in complete silence, but also in tuning into the world with purpose, filtering out the noise to genuinely engage with every sound. This is the essence of mindful listening.

From the distant chirping of birds to the rhythm of a heartbeat, the world is filled with auditory wonders waiting to be discovered. Mindful listening isn't just about external sounds; it's also about tuning into one's inner voice and finding clarity amidst chaos.

This practice is more than just an exercise for the ears. It's a journey of connection, of grounding oneself in the present, and of discovering layers of reality that often go unnoticed.

In a world overwhelmed by noise, taking the time to truly listen can be the most refreshing silence of all.

Practice: Spend a few minutes in a comfortable space, focusing solely on the sounds around you. Try to identify each one and understand its origin.

Chapter 19

Explore Mindful Presence

I once read that life isn't a series of big moments, but an accumulation of tiny, seemingly insignificant ones. And to truly live is to be present in each of these moments. This philosophy gave birth to my practice of mindful presence.

It's about being wholly there, whether I'm watching a dewdrop glisten in the morning sun or feeling the texture of a handwritten letter. Every moment becomes an experience, a memory.

By being mindfully present, I've found deeper connections with people and my surroundings. It's a celebration of life in its purest form, untouched by worries of the past or the future.

This journey is more than just about awareness. It's a deliberate choice to embrace every second, to live life not in the fast lane but one beautiful moment at a time.

Practice: Choose a routine task, like washing dishes or taking a walk. Do it with complete presence, noting every sensation and detail.

Chapter 20

Practice Self-Love

For years, I searched for love and validation in the eyes of others. It was a tiring quest, often leading to disappointment. One day, it dawned on me that the love I had been searching for was always inside me.

Self-love isn't about arrogance or conceit. It's about acknowledging one's worth, flaws and all. By embracing every facet of myself, I began to radiate confidence, warmth, and genuine happiness.

This journey of self-love was transformative. It taught me the importance of self-care, self-respect, and self-worth. I became my own best friend, cheerleader, and confidante. Life became a dance of joy, grace, and unabashed love.

Practice: Stand in front of a mirror today. Look into your eyes and list out five things you genuinely love about yourself. Say them aloud and embrace the warmth of self-appreciation.

Chapter 21

Harness the Power of Dawn Meditation

There's a magic in the early morning hours, a stillness that's unparalleled. While I've always cherished quiet mornings, introducing dawn meditation into my routine elevated the experience.

Breathing in sync with the world's waking moments, feeling the first rays of the sun, and grounding myself as the day unfolds has been incredibly rejuvenating. This practice goes beyond mere relaxation; it sets the tone for the day ahead, instilling a sense of peace and purpose.

By aligning my inner rhythms with the world outside during these pristine hours, I've found clarity, focus, and a deeper connection to the universe.

Dawn meditation is more than just a morning ritual. It's an embrace of the new day, a celebration of possibilities, and a journey into one's innermost depths.

Practice: Wake up a little earlier than usual. Find a calm spot and meditate for a few minutes, focusing on your breath and the sensations of the early morning.

Chapter 22

Nighttime Reflection

As the twilight enveloped the sky, I began a ritual of nighttime reflection. Instead of letting the day's events fade away, I took a few moments to ponder, analyze, and express gratitude for the experiences I had.

Each night became a bridge between what was and what could be. It was a time to release any lingering stress, to celebrate the day's wins, and to learn from any missteps. This reflection allowed me to lay down with a clearer conscience and lighter heart.

The benefits were manifold. I found that I slept better, dreamt more vividly, and woke up with a renewed zest for life. Nighttime wasn't an end, but a pause, a quiet interlude before another chapter began.

Practice: Before going to bed tonight, jot down three things you're grateful for from the day. Let this gratitude be the last thought you have before you drift into sleep.

Chapter 23

Dedicate Time for Laughter

There were days when life felt overwhelmingly serious, with burdens weighing heavily on my shoulders. But in those times, I found an antidote: laughter. I made it a mission to find humor in the every day, to bask in the light-hearted moments that life presented.

Sometimes it was a silly joke, a comical memory, or just a spontaneous giggle. The sound of my laughter, genuine and unbridled, became a balm for my soul. It wasn't just about the momentary joy, but the ripples it created within, rejuvenating my spirit.

I learned that laughter wasn't frivolous. It was healing, transformative, and immensely powerful. It was a reminder that no matter how tough things got, there was always a reason to smile, to laugh, and to find joy.

Practice: Watch a short comedy clip or read a few jokes today. Let yourself laugh without reservations. Notice how it uplifts your mood and lightens your spirit.

Chapter 24

Disconnect to Reconnect (Away from Social Media)

Once upon a time, I was tethered to my devices. Notifications were a constant hum, and I found myself lost in the virtual realm, missing out on the tangible world around me. So, I decided to take a break, to disconnect from social media, even if just for a while.

The first few days were challenging. But as the digital fog lifted, I began to notice the beauty around me. Conversations became richer, moments more cherished, and the world seemed vibrant in its authenticity.

This period of disconnection became my reconnection. Reconnection with my inner self, with loved ones, and with the world in its organic form. The virtual world had its place, but it couldn't replace the magic of the real.

Practice: Designate an hour today where you'll stay off all social media platforms. Use this time to engage in a hobby, talk to a loved one, or simply relax. Notice the change in your mental state.

Chapter 25

Develop Emotional Intelligence

There was a time when I felt at the mercy of my emotions, reacting to situations without truly understanding why. Then, I began my journey into the world of emotional intelligence. Recognizing, understanding, and managing my feelings became a transformative quest.

The more I delved into it, the more I realized its importance. Not just in handling my emotions, but in understanding others. Empathy grew, conflicts reduced, and relationships deepened. It was as if I'd unlocked a secret language that had always been there, but I'd been oblivious to.

My emotional intelligence became my compass, guiding my actions and reactions. It taught me to respond, not react, and to navigate the intricate maze of human emotions with grace and understanding.

Practice: Today, try to identify and label your emotions as they arise. Instead of just feeling angry, ask yourself why. Delve deeper into understanding the root cause.

PART 2

GOALS & PRODUCTIVITY

Let me tell you something about goals. We all have them. Big or small, they light up our path and guide us. Think about the last time you scribbled down a goal, whether it was shedding those few extra pounds, finishing that intriguing book collecting dust on your shelf, or aiming for the next promotion. Sounds familiar, right? But, if you're like me, you've also experienced moments where your big plans slowly got buried under the weight of daily life.

So, here we are, in the realm of Goals & Productivity. Together, we're going to uncover the real essence of goal-setting and learn how to be productive without feeling like we're running a never-ending marathon. Trust me, being productive isn't about cramming more into our already hectic days. It's about making the minutes count, being present, and picking our battles.

I'm going to share with you some of my favorite tricks, habits, and nuggets of wisdom I've gathered over the years. Think of this as a behind-the-scenes tour of how to tackle procrastination, set crystal clear boundaries, and focus on what truly lights your fire. Ready to dive in? Let's redefine what it means to be truly productive, one day at a time.

Chapter 1

Overcome Procrastination

In the vast landscape of my ambitions, I often found pockets of inertia holding me back. Shadows of doubt, fear, and lethargy would eclipse my momentum. Yet, I decided no longer to surrender to this immobilizing force. As I fought against it, a transformative shift occurred.

I recognized that procrastination wasn't about laziness; it was more about fear of the unknown or fear of failure. It was this epiphany that helped me devise a strategy. I started breaking tasks into smaller, more manageable steps, focusing on the journey rather than the daunting end-goal.

Tackling one thing at a time, the momentum built, and the looming mountains of tasks became mere molehills. The satisfaction of crossing off tasks became my new addiction.

Practice: List down a task you've been delaying. Break it into three manageable steps. Commit to finishing step one today.

Chapter 2

Forge a Personal Growth Pathway

While the principles of lifelong learning remained dear to me, I recognized the need for a bespoke pathway tailored to my aspirations. Every individual's growth journey is unique, and acknowledging this has been transformative.

Crafting this personal growth pathway wasn't just about academic pursuits. It was about recognizing my passions, understanding my limitations, and setting milestones that resonated with my inner self.

This personalized approach to learning and growth has made the journey more fulfilling. It's no longer about chasing a generic idea of success, but about nurturing a vision that's inherently mine.

Embracing this method ensures that every step, every lesson, and every challenge is aligned with my deepest aspirations, making the process of lifelong learning a truly enriching experience.

Practice: Draft a personal growth roadmap for the next year, highlighting areas you wish to explore and skills you aim to acquire.

Chapter 3

Purge Digital Clutter (E-mails)

In the digital age, my inbox became a reflection of my mind: cluttered, overwhelming, and chaotic. The endless stream of unread emails felt like a weight on my shoulders. So, I decided to take charge and declutter my digital space.

Starting with my inbox, I set clear categories, unsubscribed from unnecessary newsletters, and prioritized essential emails. It wasn't just about organization; it was about regaining control over the digital demands on my time and attention.

As I methodically cleaned out my inbox, a sense of relief washed over me. With each deleted or archived email, I felt lighter, more in control, and incredibly satisfied.

Practice: Set aside 15 minutes today to organize and declutter your primary email inbox. Start with unsubscribing from unwanted newsletters.

Chapter 4

Monitor Your Progress

At the heart of my aspirations, I sometimes felt lost, unsure of how far I'd come or how far I had to go. This ambiguity often led to frustration. Determined to change this, I began to track my progress, marking each milestone, no matter how small.

With each recorded achievement, my confidence grew. It was no longer about the destination but the journey and recognizing the strides I'd made along the way. Every step forward, every hurdle crossed, became a testament to my perseverance and growth.

As I reviewed my progress over weeks and months, the bigger picture became clear. The path I'd traveled was filled with successes, learning experiences, and moments of sheer determination.

Practice: Start a progress journal. Note down a recent achievement, however minor, and reflect on the steps that led you there.

Chapter 5

App Decluttering

Once infatuated with every new app that promised productivity or entertainment, my phone became a maze of icons. One day, I paused to consider how many of these apps truly added value to my life. The answer was stark and clear.

Embarking on a digital decluttering spree, I began removing apps that no longer served a purpose or distracted me from my goals. Each deletion felt like shedding unnecessary baggage.

With fewer apps, my phone became a tool of efficiency rather than a distraction. The simplicity not only boosted my productivity but also reduced the digital noise that had become a constant in my life.

Practice: Evaluate the apps on your phone today. Uninstall at least three that you haven't used in the past three months.

Chapter 6

Manage Digital Distractions

Drowning in the digital sea of notifications, messages, and updates, I felt perpetually distracted. These constant pings pulled me away from moments of focus and clarity. Hungry for change, I began to set boundaries with my devices.

Designating specific times for checking social media, turning off non-essential notifications, and even allocating tech-free hours, I took back control. The silence, initially startling, soon became a reservoir of creativity and focus.

In this newfound quiet, I reconnected with myself, undistracted and undisturbed, discovering the depth of thought and innovation that lay beneath the digital chaos.

Practice: Choose two hours today where you will turn off all non-essential notifications. Use this time for focused work or self-reflection.

Chapter 7

Simplify Your Living Space

My living space had become a reflection of my inner turmoil: cluttered, disorganized, and stifling. One day, I stood amidst the chaos and decided it was time for a change. I needed a space that breathed tranquility and simplicity.

I began the journey of decluttering, not just of physical items, but of the emotional baggage they represented. Each discarded item felt like releasing a piece of the past that no longer served me.

In the end, my space became a sanctuary, echoing the calm and clarity I sought within. It reminded me daily of the power of simplicity and the peace it brings.

Practice: Choose one area of your living space to declutter today. Remove at least five items that you no longer need or use.

Chapter 8

Visualize Success

Amid my ambitions and dreams, I sometimes found it challenging to believe in their fruition. That's when I turned to visualization. Closing my eyes, I painted a vivid picture of my success, feeling every emotion, every triumph.

This wasn't mere daydreaming. It was an active manifestation of my goals. By consistently visualizing my successes, they started feeling tangible, and achievable. This mental rehearsal bolstered my confidence and determination.

Now, whenever doubts creep in, I retreat to my visualization, drawing strength and inspiration from the success I've already experienced in my mind.

Practice: Spend 10 minutes today visualizing a goal you want to achieve. Immerse yourself fully in the feelings of success.

Chapter 9

Map Out Your Vision

While I had dreams, I lacked direction. Floating adrift on the sea of aspirations, I needed a map. So, I sat down and charted out my vision, breaking it into achievable segments and defining clear paths.

This roadmap became my guide, providing clarity and direction. Every decision, every choice, was now aligned with this vision. The nebulous cloud of dreams now had structure and purpose.

With a clear vision, I found purpose in each day, knowing that every step, no matter how small, was leading me towards my dreams.

Practice: Dedicate 20 minutes to map out a vision for one area of your life. Break it down into smaller, actionable steps.

Chapter 10

Create Your Vision Board

To bring my dreams to life, I decided to create a tangible representation: a vision board. This board, filled with images, quotes, and reminders of my aspirations, became a daily source of inspiration and motivation.

Every morning, glancing at this board reinforced my commitment to my goals. It served as a constant reminder of where I was headed and the life I was working towards.

Over time, as I achieved certain milestones, they found their place on the board too. It became a living testament to my journey, my challenges, and my triumphs.

Practice: Start creating your vision board today. Begin by collecting three images or quotes that resonate with your dreams.

Chapter 11

Tune into Your Inner Voice

In the cacophony of external voices – society, friends, family – I often lost track of my own. One day, amidst the noise, I paused to listen intently to my inner voice, my true self.

This inner dialogue, often subdued by external pressures, held profound insights and wisdom. By regularly tuning in, I began making decisions more in sync with my authentic self.

Listening to my inner voice didn't mean ignoring external advice. Instead, it was about striking a balance, ensuring that my path was genuinely reflective of who I was and what I desired.

Practice: Set aside 10 minutes today for quiet reflection. Listen to your thoughts and feelings without judgment.

Chapter 12

Become a Value Generator

Once a passive participant in life, I decided to shift gears. I didn't want to just consume; I wanted to contribute, to generate value. With this mindset, my approach to life transformed.

Whether in personal relationships, work, or community, I sought ways to add value. This wasn't about grand gestures but daily acts of kindness, sharing knowledge, or simply being present.

By becoming a value generator, my relationships deepened, my work became more fulfilling, and I felt a profound sense of purpose. I realized that true fulfillment comes not from what we get, but from what we give.

Practice: Identify one way you can add value to someone's life today. Act on it.

Chapter 13

Celebrate Achievements

In my relentless pursuit of the next milestone, I often overlooked the summits I had already conquered. But then, I chose to pause and honor every accomplishment, no matter how small.

This ritual of celebration became a fuel, energizing my spirit and reaffirming my capabilities. Each celebration was a testament to my resilience, determination, and hard work.

Taking a moment to bask in the joy of achievement transformed my journey. Instead of a never-ending marathon, it became a series of sprints, each ending in jubilation and rejuvenation.

Practice: Reflect on a recent achievement. Take a moment today to celebrate it, whether it's through a treat, a moment of relaxation, or simply acknowledging yourself.

Chapter 14

Prioritize Passion Projects

For so long, I had shelved my passions, placing practicality and routine above them. But, a dormant desire stirred within, urging me to reconnect with what truly ignited my spirit.

By prioritizing my passion projects, life took on a vibrant hue. These projects were not chores; they were an extension of my very soul, bringing unparalleled joy and fulfillment.

The more I engaged with what I loved, the more enriched my life became. It was a reminder that while duty and responsibility have their place, passion is the spark that sets the soul alight.

Practice: Dedicate 30 minutes today to a project or hobby you're passionate about. Let yourself be fully immersed in the joy it brings.

Chapter 15

Nourish Your Subconscious

Deep within me, beneath layers of daily distractions and surface-level thoughts, lay a reservoir of untapped wisdom – my subconscious. For a long time, it was a space I inadvertently ignored, feeding it inadvertently with stray thoughts, worries, and doubts.

But once I realized its power, I began actively nourishing it. Through affirmations, meditations, and intentional reflections, I fed it the positivity and clarity it craved. This deep mind, in return, became a guide, offering intuition, insights, and creative sparks when I least expected.

In these quiet recesses, I discovered a wellspring of understanding and vision that I never knew I possessed. It reminded me of the profound power of the mind, and the importance of curating its content.

Practice: Tonight, before you drift off to sleep, repeat an uplifting affirmation or meditate on a positive visualization. Trust in the power of your subconscious to process and magnify this.

Chapter 16

Dedicate Early Morning Self-Time

For years, my mornings were a blur of hurried routines, lost in the chaos of starting another day. But one day, I chose differently. I decided to reclaim the dawn, dedicating the first hour to myself.

The transformation was profound. The early morning, with its tranquil stillness and fresh promise, became a sanctuary. This was my time for reflection, meditation, or simply to breathe and be. Instead of charging into the day, I began greeting it with calm and intention.

With this shift, not only did my days begin on a positive note, but the quality of my entire day improved. It underscored the importance of starting right.

Practice: Tomorrow, rise just 30 minutes earlier. Spend this time in quiet reflection, a hobby, or any activity that nurtures your soul.

Chapter 17

Set Personal Boundaries

In my quest to be available and helpful, I often blurred lines, allowing others to unintentionally encroach on my personal space and time. It left me feeling drained, with my priorities constantly pushed aside. The solution? Personal boundaries.

Setting these boundaries was not about building walls, but about defining spaces. It was a profound act of self-respect and self-care, ensuring that while I was there for others, I was equally there for myself.

By valuing my own time, energy, and well-being, I not only enhanced my self-esteem but also fostered healthier relationships. It became clear that boundaries were bridges to balance and well-being.

Practice: Identify one area in your life where your boundaries are often compromised. Take a moment to clearly define this boundary and, if necessary, communicate it gently to those involved.

Chapter 18

Focus on the Goal-Setting Process

I've always been goal-driven, but my focus was always on the finish line. While achievements were sweet, I felt a void – the journey felt mechanical. Then, I shifted my gaze from the destination to the journey itself.

I started to value the process – the learning curves, the setbacks turned lessons, the small victories along the way. These became as valuable, if not more than the final achievement.

By cherishing the journey, my approach to goals transformed. They were no longer just targets but experiences, rich with growth and insights. I realized that true success lay not just in achieving a goal, but in the person I became along the way.

Practice: Consider a goal you're working towards. Instead of stressing about the outcome, take a moment today to appreciate how far you've come and the growth you've experienced.

Chapter 19

Shield from Negativity

Life, with its ebb and flow, brought its fair share of negativity. Whether from external sources or internal doubts, these negative energies had a way of clouding my vision and spirit. Determined to change this, I sought ways to shield myself.

Through positive affirmations, uplifting readings, and surrounding myself with optimistic influences, I built my protective shield. It wasn't about ignoring negativity but about reinforcing my positive defenses against it.

This proactive approach made me resilient. I could face challenges with a balanced perspective, ensuring that negativity was merely a passing cloud and not an overshadowing storm.

Practice: Think of a negative influence or thought pattern in your life. Counteract it today with a positive action or affirmation, fortifying your mental and emotional defenses.

Chapter 20

Achieve Work-Life Harmony

Juggling professional demands with personal desires, I often found myself on a tightrope, struggling to balance. Until I realized, it wasn't about balancing but harmonizing.

Achieving work-life harmony meant understanding that both facets were integral to my holistic well-being. Instead of viewing them in isolation, I sought ways to integrate them, ensuring neither was compromised.

By respecting both my professional commitments and personal needs, I crafted a life where each enriched the other. It wasn't a trade-off but a symphony, with both parts playing their roles to perfection.

Practice: Reflect on your current work-life dynamic. Identify one change you can make this week to move closer to harmony, and commit to implementing it.

Chapter 21

Feed Your Curiosity

"Curiosity will conquer fear even more than bravery will." - James Stephens

In the course of my life, I've realized that the boundaries of my knowledge are not fixed. Just when I felt I knew all there was to a subject, a fresh perspective or a novel piece of information would ignite the flames of my curiosity. By nature, we are all inquisitive creatures, yearning to understand the world and our place in it. Curiosity has always been the bridge between what I knew and what lay just beyond my understanding.

Research from the University of California suggests that being curious can help with better memory retention, especially in environments filled with distractions. The novelty of exploring and understanding something new can indeed act as a brain booster. As I began to lean into this natural desire for discovery, not only did my horizons expand, but the process of learning became more exhilarating.

But, how does one ensure they never suppress this curiosity, especially in a world with so many immediate answers? The trick lies in asking questions, constantly and consistently. Even if the answers are just a Google search away, the act of inquiry is itself a powerful tool for growth.

Practice: Dedicate 30 minutes today to delve into a topic you know little about. Make a list of questions and seek their answers, enjoying the journey of discovery.

Chapter 22
Abandon Perfectionism

Once, I was ensnared in the chains of perfectionism, feeling a compelling need to get everything just right. Over time, however, I grasped that chasing this elusive perfection only left me exhausted and often disappointed. By aiming for perfection, I was inadvertently stifling my growth and creativity, too afraid of making mistakes or facing criticism.

A study from York University found that perfectionists tend to have higher stress levels, which can lead to a host of health issues. Recognizing this, I slowly learned to cherish the journey, embracing the flaws and imperfections that made my experiences genuine and enriching.

It's not about lowering standards, but rather understanding that mistakes and setbacks are integral to growth and evolution. Letting go of perfectionism was akin to shedding a heavy burden, freeing me to take risks, experiment, and truly innovate.

Practice: Today, identify one task where you tend to seek perfection. Consciously allow yourself to complete it without overthinking. Embrace the outcome, irrespective of its flaws.

Chapter 23

Seek Assistance When Needed

Throughout my journey, pride often acted as a barrier, preventing me from seeking help even when I was overwhelmed. However, every time I did muster the courage to ask, I was pleasantly surprised by the generosity and wisdom of those around me.

Data from the Harvard Business Review indicates that individuals who seek feedback and assistance tend to progress faster in their careers. The act of reaching out not only helps in overcoming immediate challenges but also fosters deeper connections with peers and mentors.

Recognizing this, I made a conscious effort to overcome my hesitation. Seeking assistance became not an admission of weakness, but rather a testament to my commitment to personal growth and excellence.

Practice: Reflect upon a current challenge or obstacle. Reach out to someone you trust, discussing the issue and seeking their insights or suggestions.

Chapter 24

Discover the Power of Silence

"In the quiet, I have started to recognize the sound of my own voice and the desires of my own heart." –Shauna Niequist

Amidst the cacophony of modern life, silence began to seem like an unattainable luxury. But, once I consciously sought moments of quietude, the transformative power of silence became evident. It allowed introspection, clarity, and a profound connection to my inner self.

A study published in the journal "Heart" suggests that silent moments can reduce stress, releasing tension from both the mind and body. Silence, I learned, is more than the mere absence of noise. It's a space where one can heal, contemplate, and find peace.

These pockets of silence, whether in the early morning hours or during a midday break, became my sanctuary, offering respite and rejuvenation in an otherwise bustling life.

Practice: Allocate 10 minutes today, preferably in a quiet space. Sit comfortably and immerse yourself in the silence, focusing solely on your breathing.

Chapter 25

Master the Art of Time Blocking

"Time is what we want most, but what we use worst." - William Penn

Juggling myriad responsibilities, I often felt time slipping through my fingers, each day ending with a sense of unfulfillment. That's when I discovered time blocking – a practice where one allocates specific blocks of time for particular activities or tasks.

Research from the University of California, Irvine, suggests that frequent task-switching can reduce productivity by up to 40%. With time blocking, I was not only structuring my day but also ensuring that my focus remained undivided during each block.

This technique revolutionized my productivity. No longer was I at the mercy of endless to-do lists; instead, I took command of my time, ensuring that each day was both productive and fulfilling.

Practice: Examine your tasks for tomorrow. Allocate specific blocks of time for each task, ensuring you also schedule short breaks in between. Stick to these blocks as closely as possible.

PART 3

SELF-EDUCATION HABITS

It was on a cozy Sunday afternoon when I stumbled upon an old diary from my school days. Flipping through its pages, I was instantly transported back to the time when learning meant cramming dates of historical events, solving algebraic equations, and diving deep into classic literature. However, as the years went by, I realized that education wasn't limited to just textbooks or formal classes. In fact, some of the most profound lessons I've learned have come from unexpected corners of life.

Real education, as I've come to understand, doesn't stop when you walk across a graduation stage or get that fancy certificate. It's an ongoing journey, a lifelong commitment to broadening one's horizons and nurturing that innate sense of curiosity we all possess. As the world rapidly changes around us, it's our self-education habits that keep us agile, relevant, and forever growing.

The importance of these habits hit me hardest during a vacation to Cape Town. I met an old painter named Nikos who lived by the sea. With deep-set eyes and a jovial spirit, he shared tales of how he taught himself different painting techniques from various cultures just by observing, reading, and practicing. He didn't have any formal training in art, yet his house was adorned with masterpieces that could rival any great artist. His dedication to self-education was awe-inspiring, and it made me reflect on my own habits.

Every time I picked up a book not because it was required, but out of genuine interest, I was taking a step toward self-education. Those random online courses I enrolled in, the podcasts I tuned into during my morning runs and even the deep conversations with strangers – all contributed to my learning. What's more, they made the journey enjoyable and personalized.

In this section, I'm thrilled to share with you habits that will redefine the way you look at education. Think about it - we live in a digital age where knowledge isn't just confined to brick-and-mortar classrooms. It's at our fingertips, waiting for us to seize it. Whether it's picking up a new language, understanding the intricacies of the universe, or simply learning how to bake a perfect sourdough bread, there's so much out there to dive into.

As we delve into these self-education habits, I invite you to keep an open heart and mind. Remember Nikos and countless others who found wisdom not just in structured classes, but in the simple, everyday moments. Let's embark on this exciting journey of endless learning, discovery, and personal growth. After all, as the saying goes, "Live as if you were to die tomorrow. Learn as if you were to live forever."

So, are you ready to awaken that eternal student within you? Let's dive in.

Chapter 1

Dive into Genre Exploration

Reading has always been a sanctuary. But I realized that in my comfort zone, I was missing out on a myriad of worlds. Thus began my journey of genre exploration in literature.

From the mystique of sci-fi to the depths of historical fiction, every genre opened up new horizons, new perspectives. It wasn't just about the stories; it was about understanding diverse cultures, timelines, and thought processes.

This exploration was like traveling without moving, experiencing different epochs, and understanding humanity through various lenses. Each book, each genre added layers to my perspective, making me more receptive and empathetic.

The adventure of genre exploration is not just about expanding one's library but about broadening one's understanding of the world and its myriad narratives.

Practice: Each month, pick a genre you've never explored before and read at least one book from it.

Chapter 2

Finish Every Book You Start

There's a unique satisfaction in reaching the last page of a book. It signifies the end of a journey, a voyage that you embarked on with the author. But the journey isn't always smooth. There have been times when, halfway through a book, the narrative didn't resonate, or the writing style jarred. The temptation to abandon it grew.

Yet, I found merit in perseverance. By pushing through, even when the going got tough, I often discovered insights in the unlikeliest of places. Sometimes, the latter half of a book would unexpectedly captivate me. Other times, even if the narrative didn't grip me throughout, the act of finishing taught me about commitment and the value of seeing things through.

Furthermore, there's an invaluable lesson in exposing oneself to diverse perspectives. By finishing every book I start, I force myself to engage with ideas that I might not instinctively gravitate towards. It's a practice in patience, open-mindedness, and, often, in challenging my own preconceived notions.

In an age where information is abundant, and our attention spans are shrinking, the act of finishing a book becomes even more significant. It's a testament to the depth of engagement, a counteraction to the surface-level skimming that's becoming commonplace.

Practice: Revisit a book you left unfinished. Read it cover to cover, making notes on any new insights or shifts in perspective you experience.

Chapter 3

Designate TV-Free Days

Television, with its myriad shows and instantaneous news updates, has its merits. It informs, entertains, and sometimes, even educates. However, I realized that the hours I spent in front of the TV were hours I wasn't spending on other enriching activities. The passive consumption often left me feeling more drained than relaxed.

So, I decided to experiment with TV-free days. The difference was palpable. Suddenly, evenings were filled with activities that had been sidelined: reading, writing, playing board games, or simply having meaningful conversations with family members. The house seemed calmer, the environment more conducive to genuine connection.

Moreover, without the constant hum of the TV in the background, my mind felt clearer. Ideas flowed more freely, and the quality of my thoughts improved. It was as if by muting the external noise, I'd given my internal voice a chance to be heard.

Of course, the goal isn't to demonize television but to strike a balance. By consciously deciding to turn off the TV on certain days, I'm not just regulating screen time but reclaiming my time, redirecting it towards activities that add more value and meaning to my life.

Practice: Start with one designated TV-free day a week. Use this time to indulge in hobbies, activities, or simple relaxation methods you've been neglecting.

Chapter 4

Celebrate Educational Milestones

Throughout my journey, I realized that celebrating milestones wasn't just about acknowledging achievements. It was about reinforcing the joy of learning, recognizing effort, and setting the stage for future endeavors. Each milestone, no matter how small, became a testament to my commitment and perseverance.

Marking these moments added a layer of motivation. It was a reminder of the path traveled and the wonders of the journey ahead. From finishing a challenging book to mastering a complex concept, each celebration infused my educational path with enthusiasm and energy.

Practice: Reflect on your recent learning achievements, be it finishing a course, reading a set number of books, or understanding a difficult concept. Take a moment to celebrate it - maybe with a treat, a day off, or by sharing it with friends and family.

Chapter 5

The Challenge with Foreign Language Reading

Learning a new language is often likened to unlocking a door to another world. It provides a fresh lens to perceive and interact with diverse cultures and their nuances. Reading in a foreign language, though, elevates this experience. Initially, I found it arduous, grappling with unfamiliar scripts and structures. Yet, as I persisted, a beautiful transformation occurred.

Not only was I understanding the language, but I was also diving deep into the psyche, humor, and ethos of its native speakers. This deepened my empathy, enabling me to connect more profoundly with individuals from that culture.

Furthermore, tackling a foreign language has cognitive benefits. It enhances brain functionality, improves memory, and sharpens multitasking skills. It's a challenge, but one that offers immense intellectual and emotional rewards.

I chose Spanish. How about you?

Practice: Choose a beginner's book in a foreign language. Commit to reading a page or two daily, using a dictionary or translation app for assistance. Note down new vocabulary and aim to use them in sentences.

Chapter 6

Convert Commutes into Learning Time (Podcasts)

We often view commuting as a daily chore, a necessary but unproductive interval in our routine. However, with the advent of podcasts, these intervals can become treasure troves of knowledge. When I first replaced my usual music playlists with informative podcasts, the transformation was instantaneous.

Instead of passively passing time, I was actively learning, laughing, or even getting inspired. Topics ranged from history to tech innovations, from philosophical debates to quirky anecdotes. This simple shift transformed a previously "wasted" slot into a highly anticipated learning session.

By the time I reached my destination, I was not just physically relocated; my mind had journeyed through ideas and stories, leaving me more enriched than before.

Practice: Explore a podcast platform and subscribe to two or three podcasts that pique your interest. Make it a point to listen to at least one episode during your next commute.

Chapter 7

Cultivate a Growth Mindset Journal

The quest for personal development led me to create a Growth Mindset Journal. Unlike other journals focused purely on introspection, this one was all about evolution. It wasn't just about chronicling life but about finding the silver linings and lessons in every experience.

Every mistake, every setback, every "failure" was an opportunity. I began to view them not as endpoints but as invaluable feedback. And, within the pages of this journal, these errors transformed into stepping stones towards a better version of myself.

Documenting this journey shifted my perspective. It made me more resilient, more adaptable, and more open to life's ebb and flow. Because in every challenge, I now saw a lesson; in every obstacle, an opportunity.

Creating a Growth Mindset Journal is more than just writing. It's an act of transforming oneself, reshaping setbacks into setups for future success, and turning every adversity into an advantage.

Practice: At the close of your day, take a moment to reflect and write down an error or mishap and the insight you gained from it.

Chapter 8

Set a Weekly Reading Goal

Reading has always been a gateway to other worlds, a way to live multiple lives in one lifetime. But with the distractions of modern life, setting aside time for reading can be challenging. I combated this by setting a weekly reading goal. Not only did it ensure I was consistently reading, but it also transformed my reading habits.

Whether it was fiction that expanded my empathy or non-fiction that enhanced my knowledge, setting tangible targets made the experience more structured. Over time, this approach fostered a habit, ensuring reading became an integral part of my life.

No longer was I just reading; I was evolving, one book at a time.

Practice: Determine your average reading speed and set a realistic weekly goal, such as 50 pages or a chapter a day. Keep a log and track your progress, rewarding yourself when milestones are reached.

Chapter 9

Approach Education with Open-mindedness

In the journey of life, learning is a constant companion. From the early days of school to navigating adulthood, education's role is paramount. But true learning doesn't emerge from rote memorization; it blossoms from open-mindedness. I realized that when I began approaching subjects without preconceived notions, the depth of understanding deepened considerably.

Prejudices and biases, often unknowingly, cloud our judgment and distort the learning process. Being open-minded means being receptive to diverse ideas, even if they challenge our core beliefs. This receptivity not only enriches our knowledge base but also fosters intellectual humility.

Engaging in debates, discussions, and discourses with an open mind often leads to surprising revelations. It's akin to shedding layers of ignorance, revealing the core of true knowledge beneath.

Practice: The next time you're introduced to a new concept or perspective, resist the urge to judge immediately. Instead, seek to understand, ask questions, and genuinely listen to responses.

Chapter 10

Draft a Personal Learning Plan

Structure and intent are the backbones of any endeavor. This is true for learning as well. I discovered that having a tangible plan in place significantly enhanced my educational pursuits. This personal learning plan served as both a roadmap and a compass, guiding my steps in the vast ocean of knowledge.

Outlining goals, setting timelines, identifying resources – these became integral components of my plan. And as weeks turned into months, this structured approach bore fruit. Not only was I learning more, but the quality of my learning also improved.

Such a plan can be tailored and tweaked as one progresses, accommodating new interests and discarding outdated ones. It serves as a tangible testament to one's commitment to lifelong learning.

Practice: Set aside an hour this week to outline your personal learning plan. Start with broader goals and then break them down into achievable tasks with clear timelines.

Chapter 11

Embracing Journaling as a Knowledge Companion

Journaling has always felt like conversing with an old friend. Each time I open a new page, it's an opportunity to record thoughts, experiences, and reflections, offering me a canvas to document my learning journey.

As I journeyed deeper into self-education, I realized that journaling not only captures knowledge but also helps in processing it. It's a space to ask questions, record aha moments, and navigate through the maze of new information. Over time, my journal became a repository of insights, sparking connections between different ideas and fostering deeper comprehension.

There's an undeniable sense of empowerment in translating thoughts into words on paper. It gives them life and solidity. Journaling is more than mere documentation; it's a ritual of understanding, a dance between the conscious and subconscious, making the abstract tangible.

Practice: Dedicate 10 minutes each evening to journal about what you've learned throughout the day. Note down key insights, lingering questions, and how the new information resonates with your existing knowledge.

Chapter 12

Embrace the Joy of Continuous Learning

Life itself is a classroom, where every day presents an opportunity to learn something new. However, amidst the hustle and bustle, we sometimes forget the sheer joy that continuous learning brings. From the elation of discovering a new topic to the thrill of connecting disparate ideas, there's a unique pleasure in being a lifelong learner.

As a child, the world seemed vast and endlessly mysterious. Every experience was an opportunity to grasp something novel. Somehow, as we grew older, this sense of wonder often diminished, overshadowed by routines and responsibilities. But the truth is, the joy of learning never truly leaves us; it only waits for us to rediscover it.

Dedicating oneself to continuous learning isn't just about gaining knowledge; it's also about keeping our minds agile, curious, and young. Whether it's picking up a new hobby, reading a challenging article, or simply conversing with someone from a different background, every experience can be a lesson.

Practice: Start a 'Lifelong Learning' diary. Dedicate a few minutes at the end of each day to write about something new you've learned, no matter how small or big. Reflect on this diary every weekend, relishing the journey of endless discovery.

Chapter 13

Review and Reflect on Learnings

Every so often, it's essential to pause and look back. I found that reflection is as crucial to the learning process as the acquisition of knowledge itself. When I took time to contemplate what I'd learned, the lessons solidified in my memory, making them easier to apply in real-life situations.

Reflection fosters depth. By reviewing the materials, concepts, or skills I'd been exposed to, I was able to discern patterns, make connections, and glean insights that weren't immediately apparent during the initial learning phase.

Moreover, this exercise highlighted areas where my understanding was lacking, pointing me towards topics that required further exploration. It was like tightening the screws of a newly assembled piece of furniture, ensuring sturdiness and longevity.

Practice: Every weekend, set aside an hour to review the most significant things you've learned during the week. Write down key insights, questions, and potential areas of further exploration.

Chapter 14

Seek and Learn from Mentors

One of the most transformative steps in my learning journey was seeking out mentors. These individuals, with their wealth of experience and knowledge, provided guidance, perspective, and sometimes, the much-needed push to venture beyond my comfort zone.

Mentors aren't just repositories of knowledge; they are navigators who have traveled the path before. Their insights into pitfalls to avoid, resources to utilize, and strategies to adopt can often fast-track one's learning process.

The beauty of mentorship lies in its reciprocity. While I absorbed knowledge from my mentors, I also brought a fresh perspective, prompting them to see things in a new light, thereby making the relationship mutually enriching.

Practice: Identify a field or skill you're passionate about and seek out potential mentors. It could be through networking, online platforms, or community groups. Initiate a conversation and express your desire to learn.

Chapter 15

Engage in Online Courses

In the digital age, the world is at our fingertips. I realized that online courses are a goldmine of knowledge, offering flexibility, diversity, and depth. From niche skills to broad academic subjects, there's a course for virtually everything.

These platforms allowed me to learn at my own pace, revisit topics when necessary, and engage with a global community of learners. The variety of teaching methodologies, from video lectures to interactive assignments, catered to different learning styles, enhancing retention and understanding.

While traditional education systems have their merits, the democratization of knowledge through online courses has been a game-changer, making lifelong learning accessible to all.

Practice: Explore platforms like Coursera, Udemy, or Khan Academy. Pick a course that piques your interest and commit to completing it within a set timeframe.

Chapter 16

Join Discussion Groups

There's a certain magic in collective learning. I discovered that joining discussion groups added a dynamic, interactive layer to my education. These forums, whether online or offline, became spaces where ideas were exchanged, debated, and refined.

Listening to diverse perspectives enhanced my understanding of subjects, and articulating my thoughts helped cement my learnings. These groups became crucibles of intellectual stimulation, where knowledge was not just acquired but actively constructed.

Moreover, the sense of community and camaraderie fostered in these groups made the learning process more enjoyable and sustainable.

Practice: Find discussion groups related to your interests on platforms like Meetup, Facebook, or local community boards. Attend a session or two and actively participate in the discussions.

Chapter 17

Attend Workshops and Seminars

Attending workshops and seminars was a game changer for me. These events provide a hands-on, immersive experience that is often hard to replicate through self-study. They allowed me to interact with experts, gain practical insights, and network with like-minded individuals.

There's a palpable energy in these settings – a collective enthusiasm for learning and growth. It's more than just acquiring knowledge; it's about experiencing it firsthand. The practical exercises, the Q&A sessions, the shared experiences – all these elements come together to create a holistic learning experience.

Moreover, these events often act as catalysts, reigniting my passion for a subject and providing fresh motivation to delve deeper. They offer a unique blend of theory and practice, ensuring that the knowledge gained is not just abstract but immediately applicable.

Practice: Research upcoming workshops or seminars in your area or online. Choose one that aligns with your interests and make a commitment to attend.

Chapter 18

Explore Educational Apps

In the age of smartphones, I recognized that learning could be seamlessly integrated into daily life. Educational apps became my go-to tools for bite-sized, on-the-go learning. From language acquisition to coding, from history to neuroscience, there's an app for virtually every domain.

These apps leverage interactive modules, gamification techniques, and personalized feedback mechanisms to make learning engaging and effective. The flexibility they offer – to learn anytime, anywhere – ensures that I can utilize pockets of free time throughout the day.

It's not just about convenience; it's about consistency. With these apps, I could maintain a daily learning streak, ensuring steady progress and retention.

Practice: Explore your app store for top-rated educational apps in your field of interest. Download one and set aside 10 minutes each day for a learning session.

Chapter 19

Documentary Dive-In

Documentaries opened up a world of in-depth exploration for me. They provide a visual journey into a subject, combining narrative, research, and visuals to offer a comprehensive overview. Whether it was about nature, historical events, scientific discoveries, or societal issues, documentaries enriched my understanding in ways that books or articles sometimes couldn't.

The immersive experience, backed by visuals and expert interviews, offered a multidimensional perspective. It's like taking a deep dive into a subject, coming out with nuanced insights and a broader understanding.

Besides knowledge, documentaries often stirred emotions, prompting introspection, empathy, and sometimes, action. They have the power to inform, inspire, and ignite change.

Practice: Choose a topic you're curious about and find a highly-rated documentary on it. Set a date and time for a viewing session, and immerse yourself fully.

Chapter 20

Curate a Personal Library

Books have always been treasured companions for me. Over time, I realized the importance of curating a personal library – a collection of books that inspire, challenge, and guide. Each book, carefully chosen, became a testament to my intellectual journey, representing phases, interests, and milestones.

Having a personal library meant that knowledge was always within arm's reach. On days when I sought inspiration, solace, or guidance, I'd pick a book from my shelf, finding answers and perspectives within its pages.

Moreover, the very act of curating – of selecting books with care and intention – enhanced my engagement with the content. Each addition became a deliberate choice, a nod to my commitment to lifelong learning.

Practice: Set aside a space in your home for your personal library. Start with a few essential books in your field of interest and gradually expand, adding titles that resonate with your learning journey.

PART 4

PHYSICAL HEALTH HABITS

Imagine waking up every day with a burst of energy, your body in sync with your mind, ready to face whatever challenges come your way. When I started focusing on my physical well-being, it wasn't just my body that transformed; my mindset did too. I realized that our physical health isn't just about looking a certain way, but about feeling a certain way. It's about harnessing energy, building resilience, and fostering a harmony between body and mind that benefits every aspect of our lives.

Over the years, I've dabbled in various diets, joined and quit multiple gym memberships, and tried countless wellness trends. But what I've come to understand is that genuine physical health isn't rooted in short-term goals or passing fads. It's about establishing consistent, sustainable habits that become as natural as breathing. It's about listening to our bodies, understanding its needs, and nurturing it with care and intention.

Each of us has a unique body, with individual needs and preferences. What works wonders for one person might not be suitable for another. That's why it's crucial to approach physical health with an open mind, willing to experiment, learn, and adapt. The habits we'll dive into in this section are not prescriptive rules but suggestions and springboards to inspire your personal journey towards optimal physical health.

Remember that each small choice you make can compound over time. Drinking that extra glass of water, taking the stairs instead of the elevator, or dedicating just ten minutes a day for stretching might seem insignificant in isolation. However, when repeated daily, they lay the foundation for a vibrant, energetic, and healthy life.

Embracing physical health habits is not just an act of self-care; it's a statement of self-respect. By investing time and energy into our bodies, we're acknowledging its worth and its role in shaping our overall well-being. As we venture into this section, I invite you to approach each habit with curiosity and compassion, finding the perfect balance that resonates with your lifestyle and aspirations.

Chapter 7

Minimize Sugar Intake

We've all been there: the mid-afternoon energy slump that has us reaching for a sugary treat. And while there's nothing wrong with indulging occasionally, consistently high sugar intake can have adverse effects on our health. Sugar, especially the refined kind, can lead to weight gain, dental issues, and even more severe health problems like diabetes. But more than that, it can become a crutch, an instant source of energy that our body begins to rely on, only to crash later.

I began to notice how sluggish I felt after binging on sugary foods. My energy levels would peak and then drop dramatically, leaving me tired and irritable. It became clear that minimizing sugar was more than just a diet choice; it was a way to ensure sustained energy and a clearer mind throughout the day.

Practice: Start by checking the nutritional information of your go-to snacks. Try replacing one sugary treat a day with a healthier alternative. Maybe a piece of fruit or a handful of nuts? Small steps can lead to big changes.

Chapter 2

Prioritize Restful Sleep

Let me tell you, there's a vast difference between lying in bed for eight hours and getting a full, restful eight hours of sleep. Sleep is when our body heals, processes the events of the day, and recharges for what's ahead. I learned the hard way that skimping on sleep can make me feel foggy-headed, irritable, and just not at my best.

Recall those nights when you experienced deep, undisturbed rest? You wake up feeling refreshed, rejuvenated, and ready to tackle the day. It's not just about the quantity but the quality of sleep.

Creating a bedtime routine, minimizing screen time before bed, and ensuring your sleeping environment is comfortable are all essential components of restful sleep.

Practice: Tonight, try setting a bedtime alarm to remind you to wind down. Consider reading a book or practicing some light stretches to signal your body that it's time to rest.

Chapter 3

Stay Consistently Hydrated

It's incredible how many of us move through our day in a state of mild dehydration without even realizing it. Our bodies are mostly water, and even a slight dip in hydration levels can lead to feelings of fatigue, dry skin, and headaches. When I started focusing on my hydration levels, I felt a clear difference in my energy levels and overall well-being.

Keep a water bottle handy throughout the day. If plain water isn't your thing, try infusing it with slices of fruit or herbs for a refreshing twist. Regular hydration not only keeps our body functioning optimally but also helps in flushing out toxins.

Practice: Aim to drink at least eight glasses of water today. Keep track and notice how you feel when you meet your hydration goals.

Chapter 4

Incorporate Planks in Fitness Routine

Ah, the humble plank. It may look simple, but this exercise is a powerhouse. Not only does it strengthen your core, but it also works out multiple muscle groups simultaneously. I incorporated planks into my routine and soon felt stronger, more balanced, and saw an improvement in my posture.

The beauty of the plank is its versatility. It can be done anywhere, anytime, and doesn't require any equipment. Plus, there are many variations to try, ensuring you won't quickly get bored.

Practice: Start with a 20-second plank today. Focus on form: keep your body straight and engage your core. Gradually increase your time as you get stronger.

Chapter 5

Strengthen with Push-ups

Push-ups, in my opinion, are one of the most underrated exercises. They're often associated with rigorous military training, but in reality, push-ups are fantastic for strengthening the upper body and core. When I first started, I could barely do a couple without feeling the strain. But with time and consistency, I built strength and endurance.

There are various forms of push-ups, from the classic style to knee push-ups, that can cater to different fitness levels. The key is to start where you are and focus on improving bit by bit.

Practice: Try doing three sets of push-ups today, with as many repetitions as you're comfortable with. Remember to maintain proper form and alignment.

Chapter 6

Practice Kapalabhati Breathing

Breathing, something so natural and automatic, can transform when done with intention. Kapalabhati, often referred to as "skull shining breath" in yoga, is a practice I began to invigorate my body and mind. This rapid, forceful breathing technique can increase energy, improve digestion, and provide a sense of clarity.

Incorporating Kapalabhati into my morning routine became a game-changer. It's like giving myself a dose of natural caffeine, sans the jitters. Remember, though, it's essential to learn and practice this under guidance, especially if you're a beginner.

Practice: Start with 30 seconds of Kapalabhati breathing, ensuring you've learned the correct technique. Gradually increase the duration over time.

Chapter 7

Relish Garden Walks

Nature has a unique way of calming our minds and rejuvenating our souls. For me, taking a stroll in the garden, listening to the birds chirp, and feeling the grass beneath my feet is therapeutic. It's an instant mood lifter, a way to reconnect with nature and center myself.

No matter how busy my day gets, I make it a point to spend at least a few minutes outdoors. The fresh air, the natural beauty—it all serves as a reminder of the simple joys of life.

Practice: Dedicate 10 minutes of your day for a garden walk. If you don't have a garden, a park or any green space will do. Disconnect from technology during this time and be present in the moment.

Chapter 8

Prioritize Plant-Based Foods

Our diet plays a massive role in our overall well-being. I've always tried to maintain a balanced diet, but the real shift came when I began prioritizing plant-based foods. Fruits, vegetables, nuts, and grains are rich in essential nutrients, fiber, and antioxidants that our body thrives on.

Gradually, as I incorporated more plant-based foods into my meals, I noticed improved digestion, higher energy levels, and even better skin. It's not about completely eliminating other food groups but ensuring that plant-based foods form a significant part of your diet.

Practice: For your next meal, try filling half your plate with vegetables. Experiment with new recipes to make this shift exciting and delicious.

Chapter 9

Limit Caffeine Consumption

I love a good cup of coffee just as much as the next person. But over time, I realized that my multiple cups a day were doing more harm than good. Overconsumption of caffeine can lead to anxiety, restlessness, and sleep disturbances.

I decided to limit my caffeine intake, replacing my usual afternoon cup with herbal teas or just plain water. The initial days were challenging, but soon, my sleep improved, and I felt more at ease throughout the day.

Practice: Today, try replacing one of your caffeinated drinks with a non-caffeinated alternative. Notice how your body responds over time.

Chapter 10

Master the Art of Saying NO

Safeguarding our physical health isn't always about diet and exercise. Sometimes, it's about setting boundaries and understanding our limits. I used to be someone who said 'yes' to everything, often stretching myself thin and feeling overwhelmed.

Learning to say 'no' was liberating. It allowed me to prioritize my well-being and ensure I wasn't overcommitting. Remember, saying 'no' isn't about being selfish; it's about self-preservation.

Practice: The next time you're faced with a commitment or task that you're not up for, practice saying 'no.' It might be challenging initially, but it's a vital skill for maintaining physical and mental well-being.

PART 5

HAPPINESS

Happiness, a seemingly elusive concept, is often pictured as the grand finale of our pursuits. We chase it in our dreams, in people, in our jobs, and even in the distant corners of the world. But as I embarked on this journey of self-exploration and growth, I discovered a profound truth: happiness isn't a destination. It's a daily practice, a series of choices we make, and most importantly, a state of mind.

Many believe that happiness hinges on external factors – that it's something to be found in the right job, the perfect relationship, or perhaps in the dream home. While these can undoubtedly add joy to our lives, the foundation of genuine, lasting happiness lies within us. It's about cultivating an inner ecosystem of gratitude, mindfulness, and contentment.

In this section, "Happiness," we delve deeper into the myriad ways to tap into our reservoirs of joy. It's not about seeking happiness but about recognizing and nurturing it in our daily lives. These chapters will guide you through practices, insights, and habits that aim to amplify the happiness quotient in your life. From fostering meaningful connections to savoring life's simple pleasures, this journey promises a heartwarming exploration of what truly matters.

Let's redefine happiness. Not as a distant dream, but as an accessible, daily ritual. As we journey through this section, may you discover the many hues of happiness and recognize that the source of true joy has been within you all along.

Chapter 7

Random Acts of Kindness

We often underestimate the ripple effect of a single act of kindness. From holding the door open for someone, buying a coffee for the next person in line, to simply complimenting a friend's new hairstyle—these acts, no matter how small, can light up someone's day. In a world that sometimes feels saturated with negativity, a little kindness goes a long way. It creates a chain reaction, instilling a sense of warmth and love, not just in the receiver but also in the giver.

The beauty of random acts of kindness is their spontaneity. They come straight from the heart, without any expectations of reciprocation. They are a testament to the boundless goodness within us, and their mere act can elevate our spirits, making us feel connected to the larger tapestry of humanity.

Practice: Today, perform three random acts of kindness. It could be anything – leaving a generous tip, helping someone with their bags, or even sending a heartfelt text to a loved one. Notice how you feel after each act.

Chapter 2

Reflect on Benefactors in Life

Life's path is marked by numerous individuals who have deeply impacted our lives.Whether it's the elementary school teacher who believed in your abilities, a friend who stood by you during tough times, or even a stranger whose simple gesture left a mark — these are the unsung heroes of our stories. Taking a moment to reflect on these benefactors fosters a deep sense of gratitude and a recognition of the interconnectedness of our lives.

As I pause and think about the people who've impacted my journey, it brings forth an overwhelming sensation of warmth. This exercise is not just about acknowledging their contributions, but also about realizing that we, too, have played the role of a benefactor in someone else's story. It creates a beautiful cycle of giving and receiving, where gratitude becomes the guiding force.

Practice: Set aside 10 minutes today. Close your eyes and think of three people who've positively impacted your life. Visualize a moment you shared with them and silently express your gratitude.

Chapter 3

Cultivate a Monk Mindset

The world around us is in a constant state of flux, with distractions at every turn. Amidst this chaos, the mindset of a monk — characterized by simplicity, focus, and serenity — can be a beacon. It's not about renouncing worldly possessions but embracing a mindset of clarity and purpose. A monk mindset teaches us to prioritize what's essential, finding solace in silence, and appreciate the transient nature of everything around us.

Drawing inspiration from monks, I've learned the art of mindful living. By decluttering my thoughts, focusing on the present, and grounding myself in moments of stillness, I've unlocked an unparalleled sense of peace. It's a journey of turning inwards, recognizing the cacophonies of the outer world, but choosing not to get entangled.

Practice: Start your day with a 5-minute meditation session. Sit in a comfortable position, take deep breaths, and let go of any lingering thoughts. Embrace the calm and carry this serenity with you throughout the day.

Chapter 4

Find Joy in Everyday Life

Everyday life is filled with moments, some mundane and others monumental. But within the ordinary lies the extraordinary – moments of pure joy waiting to be discovered. From the aroma of freshly brewed coffee, the soft rays of morning sunshine, to the laughter of loved ones – joy is sprinkled everywhere, just waiting to be acknowledged.

Over the years, I've come to realize that it's these seemingly insignificant moments that string together to form the tapestry of our lives. By tuning into them, we not only amplify our daily happiness but also develop a deeper appreciation for life's simple pleasures. The magic, after all, is not always in the milestones but in the moments between.

Practice: Today, carry a small notebook with you. Jot down five moments that brought a smile to your face, no matter how trivial. Before sleeping, revisit these moments and soak in the happiness.

Chapter 5

Connect with Nature

Nature, in all its grandeur and beauty, has a therapeutic touch. The rustling of leaves, the chirping of birds, the serene waves hitting the shore – all resonate with a symphony that's both calming and invigorating. Every time I step into nature's embrace, I'm reminded of the intricate web of life and the beauty of being a part of this vast universe.

Connecting with nature isn't just about weekend getaways or vacations. It's a daily practice. Even in the most urban landscapes, pockets of greenery and tranquility await our presence. Whether it's a stroll in the park, tending to a home garden, or simply watching the sunset, nature has a way of grounding us, reminding us of life's simple wonders.

Practice: Dedicate 20 minutes to nature today. It could be watering plants, walking barefoot on grass, or even listening to the sound of rain. Absorb the sights and sounds, letting nature's serenity wash over you.

Chapter 6

Delight in Simple Joys

Life's charm often lies in its simplicity. In an era where we're inundated with the need for grandeur, it's the simple joys that offer solace. The joy of biting into a ripe fruit, the laughter shared over a silly joke or the comfort of an old song - these are the moments that infuse our days with happiness. It's not the extravagance but the essence that matters.

I've found that the key to happiness often lies in savoring these moments. By slowing down and truly experiencing these fleeting moments, we elevate our daily experiences. It's a gentle reminder that joy doesn't always have to be sought; sometimes, it's right in front of us, waiting to be relished.

Practice: Make a list of five simple joys that resonate with you. It could be the taste of your favorite ice cream or the feel of fresh sheets. Engage in one of these joys today, savoring every moment of it.

Chapter 7

Kickstart with a Morning Ritual

Mornings, often symbolizing new beginnings, have the power to set the tone for the rest of our day. A morning ritual isn't just about tasks; it's about intention. Whether it's sipping on a cup of tea, practicing yoga, or simply soaking in the silence before the world wakes up - it's these practices that ground us, offering a fresh start every day.

Over the years, I've realized the transformative power of mornings. A consistent ritual has given me a sense of purpose and direction. It's a sacred time, a moment to reconnect with myself before diving into the day's chaos. By giving myself this time, I've been able to approach my days with more clarity, enthusiasm, and positivity.

Practice: If you don't already have one, establish a simple morning ritual for yourself. Start with just one activity that you love, and commit to it for a week. Notice how it impacts the rest of your day.

Chapter 8

Welcome Fresh Ideas

Stagnation, in thoughts or routines, can often lead to a sense of monotony. It's in these moments that welcoming fresh ideas can act as a breath of fresh air. From exploring a new hobby, diving into an unfamiliar book, to even changing your daily route - these new experiences infuse our lives with excitement and novelty.

I've often found that embracing new ideas or perspectives has broadened my horizon. It's not just about novelty, but about growth. By challenging our established patterns and welcoming the unknown, we not only rejuvenate our spirits but also foster a mindset of continuous learning and curiosity.

Practice: Today, break a routine. It could be trying a new recipe, reading a genre you usually avoid, or simply rearranging your workspace. Notice how this shift invigorates your spirit.

Chapter 9

Reflect through Windows

There's something meditative about gazing out of a window. As the world unfolds outside, it provides a canvas for introspection. The changing landscapes, the ebb and flow of life – all of it acts as a mirror, reflecting our innermost thoughts and feelings.

In my moments of contemplation, windows have often been my silent companions. They've allowed me a space to pause, reflect, and often find clarity. Beyond the physical vista they offer, windows serve as a metaphorical bridge, connecting our inner and outer worlds, providing a silent refuge for our wandering thoughts.

Practice: Dedicate 10 minutes today to window-gazing. Whether you're looking at a bustling street or a tranquil garden, let your thoughts flow freely, finding solace in this quiet reflection.

Chapter 10

Relive Memories (Through Photos)

Photographs are timeless treasures, portals to moments gone by. Flipping through old albums or scrolling through digital memories, we're instantly transported to times filled with joy, nostalgia, and sometimes, even melancholy. These visual reminders aren't just about the past; they're gateways to introspection, allowing us to relive, cherish, and often, learn from our history.

In my quieter moments, I often turn to old photos. They remind me of the journey, of the highs and lows, and most importantly, of the transient nature of time. Every photo tells a story, and by revisiting them, we not only relive the past but also appreciate the present more deeply.

Practice: Today, spend some time revisiting old photographs. Dive into the emotions they evoke, reminisce about the stories they tell, and cherish the journey they represent.

Chapter 11

Revel in Reading's Magic

Books, with their myriad worlds and stories, offer an escape unlike any other. Diving into a book is like embarking on a journey, one where we're both spectators and participants. With every page turned, we not only delve into the author's universe but also discover facets of ourselves.

Over the years, I've realized that reading isn't just about the stories or information; it's a deeply introspective process. Books challenge our beliefs, offer new perspectives, and most importantly, resonate with the human experience's universality. The magic of reading lies in this connection, this silent dialogue between the reader and the written word.

Practice: Dedicate 30 minutes today to reading. It could be a novel, a magazine, or even a blog post. Delve deep into the narrative and let yourself be transported by the magic of words.

Chapter 12

Implement the 1 Minute Rule

The 1 Minute Rule is simple: if a task takes less than a minute, do it immediately. Whether it's replying to a text, washing a cup, or jotting down a thought – this simple strategy can immensely boost productivity. On the surface, it might seem trivial, but in essence, it's about momentum. By tackling these small tasks, we not only declutter our space and mind but also set the tone for larger tasks.

I've found that implementing this rule has significantly reduced my procrastination. It's not just about the tasks at hand, but the sense of accomplishment that follows. By building on these small wins, we pave the way for a more organized, efficient, and stress-free environment.

Practice: Today, consciously practice the 1 Minute Rule. Tackle those small, nagging tasks and observe how they impact your overall productivity and mood.

Chapter 13

Surround with Positivity

The company we keep significantly influences our mindset and outlook towards life. Surrounding ourselves with positive, uplifting individuals can act as a catalyst for personal growth and happiness. It's not just about avoiding negativity, but actively seeking out environments and people that inspire, motivate, and resonate with our core values.

Throughout my journey, I've realized that being selective about my surroundings has been instrumental in shaping my mindset. By choosing positivity, I've not only enhanced my personal well-being but have also become a source of inspiration for others. After all, positivity is contagious, and its ripple effect is boundless.

Practice: Reflect on your immediate circle today. Are there individuals who uplift you? Make an effort to spend more time with them. Similarly, identify any sources of negativity and consider ways to reduce their influence.

Chapter 14

Let Go of the Past

Our past, with its tapestry of experiences, forms the foundation of our present. However, clinging to past regrets, mistakes, or even successes can hinder our growth. Letting go doesn't mean forgetting or suppressing; it means acknowledging, learning, and moving forward. By releasing the weight of the past, we pave the way for a future filled with possibilities.

As I've navigated life's ups and downs, I've come to appreciate the liberating power of letting go. It's a conscious choice to not be held back by bygones, to embrace the present with open arms. Every moment offers a fresh start, and by letting go, we claim our power to shape our destiny.

Practice: Spend 15 minutes reflecting on an event from the past that still lingers in your mind. Acknowledge your feelings, learn from the experience, and then consciously choose to let it go.

Chapter 15

Strategies to Combat Overthinking

Overthinking, often termed as 'analysis paralysis', can be debilitating. It's a vortex of endless thoughts, where we replay scenarios, drown in 'what ifs', and often end up feeling overwhelmed. While introspection is healthy, excessive rumination can hinder decision-making and affect our mental well-being. It's crucial to have strategies in place to break this cycle.

Over the years, I've experimented with various techniques to combat overthinking – from mindfulness practices, and journaling, to even engaging in physical activity. The key lies in recognizing the onset of overthinking and actively redirecting our focus. By doing so, we not only alleviate undue stress but also enhance our clarity and decision-making prowess.

Practice: The next time you catch yourself overthinking, try the '5-4-3-2-1' grounding technique. Identify five things you can see, four you can touch, three you can hear, two you can smell, and one you can taste. This simple exercise can bring you back to the present moment.

Chapter 16

Embrace Uncertainties

Life, in its essence, is unpredictable. While planning and foresight have their place, it's also essential to embrace life's uncertainties. These unforeseen twists and turns, while sometimes challenging, often lead to growth and new opportunities. By surrendering to the flow, we open ourselves to experiences that might never have been part of our planned narrative.

Throughout my journey, I've realized that some of the most enriching experiences stemmed from unexpected quarters. By letting go of the need to control every outcome, I've learned to dance in the rain, celebrate the detours, and most importantly, trust the journey, knowing that every twist and turn holds a purpose.

Practice: Today, do something spontaneous. Whether it's trying out a new café, taking a different route to work, or simply engaging in a random act of kindness – let go of the script and revel in the beauty of the unplanned.

Chapter 17

Celebrate Kindness

In a world where we often race against time, we sometimes forget the power of simple acts of kindness. These acts, however small they may seem, hold the power to transform someone's day and, occasionally, their perspective. Celebrating kindness isn't just about acknowledging good deeds done towards us, but also recognizing and appreciating our capacity for compassion towards others.

Over the years, I've learned that kindness has a ripple effect. A simple smile, a genuine compliment, or even holding the door open for someone can set off a chain reaction of goodwill. Moreover, these actions don't just benefit the recipient but enrich our own souls, filling us with warmth and purpose.

Practice: Commit to performing three acts of kindness today. It can be anything from complimenting a coworker, paying for someone's coffee, or even just listening to someone who needs to talk. At the end of the day, reflect on how it made you feel.

Chapter 18

Cultivate an Optimistic Environment

It's often said that we're a product of our environment. Recognizing this, I began to actively shape mine, ensuring that it radiated optimism. This wasn't just about personal mindset; it was about the spaces, routines, and even the company I kept.

From surrounding myself with inspiring art to curating uplifting playlists, every detail mattered. But the most transformative change came from choosing to engage with individuals who radiated positivity, those who uplifted rather than brought down.

This active cultivation of an optimistic environment became a pillar of strength. In challenging times, this environment served as a sanctuary, a reminder of hope and joy.

Cultivating such an environment isn't about denying the negative but about amplifying the positive. It's about creating spaces that rejuvenate, inspire, and uplift.

Practice: Make a list of five elements in your environment that you can enhance to make it more optimistic. Work on one item each week.

Chapter 19

The Joy of Giving

The adage "It's better to give than to receive" rings true in more ways than one. Giving, be it in terms of time, resources, or even just genuine advice, not only benefits the recipient but also enriches our own lives. This joy isn't just rooted in the act itself but in the realization of the positive impact we can create.

My experiences have repeatedly shown me that in giving, I've received much more - in terms of gratitude, love, and a deep sense of fulfillment. This reciprocal cycle of goodwill and happiness underscores the interconnectedness of our journeys.

Practice: Allocate a small portion of your time or resources to a cause or individual in need this week. Notice the feelings that arise from this act and reflect on its broader implications in your life.

Chapter 20

The Healing Power of Forgiveness

Holding onto grudges or past hurts can weigh us down, often preventing us from moving forward and embracing the present. Forgiveness, in this context, isn't just about the other person; it's a gift we give ourselves. It's the act of releasing resentment, allowing us to heal, grow, and find inner peace.

Throughout life, I've encountered situations where forgiveness seemed challenging. However, with time and introspection, I've recognized that by holding onto resentment, I was only harming myself. Letting go and embracing forgiveness was my path to healing and rediscovering joy.

Practice: Reflect on a past event or individual that might still hold a grip on your emotions. Write a letter of forgiveness to them, pouring out your feelings. You don't need to send this letter; the act of writing itself is a step toward healing and letting go.

Conclusion: Embracing the Journey of Self-Discovery

As we stand at the closing pages of this journey, it's essential to pause and reflect on the distance we've traveled together. This book, which started as a roadmap for personal growth and holistic well-being, evolved into a collaborative adventure of introspection, understanding, and transformative habits. By this point, you've armed yourself with tools, techniques, and perspectives spanning diverse realms from mindfulness to physical health, from self-education to the pursuit of genuine happiness.

Every chapter was designed to be a stepping stone, a milestone to help you elevate your understanding of yourself and the world around you. We dived deep into the world of mindful growth and mental health in Part 1, exploring the richness of self-compassion, the tranquility in mindful presence, and the significance of emotional intelligence. These were not just chapters; they were invitations—invitations to look within, to observe without judgment, and to grow beyond our perceived limitations.

In Part 2, the spotlight shifted to productivity and goals. As we meandered through the corridors of personal boundaries, time management, and vision crafting, the message was clear: To achieve our dreams, we must first build them, brick by brick, with clarity, focus, and an unwavering commitment to our values. Our exploration of self-education habits in Part 3 was a testament to the power of continuous learning, the joy of discovery, and the significance of cultivating a growth mindset. After all, as the adage goes, the day we stop learning is the day we stop growing.

The journey into physical health habits in Part 4 was a reminder that our bodies are not just vessels but temples. Prioritizing rest, hydration, nutrition, and exercise isn't about aesthetics; it's about reverence for this incredible machine that carries us through life, allowing us to experience, learn, love, and grow. By nurturing our physical health, we bolster our mental and emotional well-being, closing the circle of holistic health.

Finally, in Part 5, we embraced the myriad facets of happiness. From the simplest joys to profound realizations, from cultivating positivity to letting go of past burdens, it was a section that sang the songs of the heart.

As you move forward, remember that personal growth is not a destination but a journey. It's a path laden with discoveries, challenges, joys, and learnings. The tools and habits we discussed are not checkboxes to tick off but practices to integrate, adapt, and make your own. Your journey will be as unique as your fingerprint, and that's the beauty of it.

In this conclusion, I urge you not to view this book as an ending but as a beginning. A beginning of a journey you commit to every day, every moment. So, take this book, revisit its pages when you need a gentle reminder, share its wisdom with others, and most importantly, live its teachings.

Your final takeaway: **Commit to growth, not perfection**. Every day offers a new opportunity to be a slightly better version of who you were yesterday. Cherish the journey, embrace the learnings, and remember that in the pursuit of personal growth, the journey is the reward.

Thank you for embarking on this adventure with me. May your path be filled with insights, joy, and boundless growth. Onwards and upwards!

www.ingramcontent.com/pod-product-compliance
Lightning Source LLC
LaVergne TN
LVHW091053150826

845673LV00002B/562

9798891333833